TRANSGENDER PIONEERS

CHAZ BONO

MARTIN GITLIN

ROSEN PUBLISHING

Published in 2017 by The Rosen Publishing Group, Inc.
29 East 21st Street, New York, NY 10010

Copyright © 2017 by The Rosen Publishing Group, Inc.

First Edition

Library of Congress Cataloging-in-Publication Data

Names: Gitlin, Marty, author.
Title: Chaz Bono / Martin Gitlin.
Description: First edition. | New York, NY : Rosen Publishing Group,
Inc., 2017. | Series: Transgender pioneers | Includes bibliographical
references and index.
Identifiers: LCCN 2015047415 | ISBN 9781508171577 (library bound)
Subjects: LCSH: Bono, Chaz—Juvenile literature. | Transgender
people—United States—Biography—Juvenile literature. |
Transsexuals—United States—Biography—Juvenile literature.
Classification: LCC HQ77.8.B66 G57 2016 | DDC 306.76/8092—dc23
LC record available at http://lccn.loc.gov/2015047415

Manufactured in China

CONTENTS

Chaz Bono is photographed smiling at the 25th Annual GLAAD Media Awards on April 12, 2014.

For Chaz Bono, life has been a bumpy journey filled with many struggles and remarkable triumphs. As the son of celebrity parents Sonny and Cher, Chaz's childhood was no walk in the park. Frequent moves, an unstable home environment, and his parents' highly publicized divorce made for a challenging upbringing. Throughout his teenage years and much of his adult life, Bono suffered from depression as he came to terms with his sexual orientation and gender identity. His path to happiness was made all the more difficult because it was charted in the public eye. As the son of legendary entertainers, his every move has drawn media attention.

As a young child, Chaz could internally sense that he was a boy (Chaz had been assigned female at birth). His mother and his overbearing nanny both pushed him into behaving more "like a girl" and wearing dresses and other clothes traditionally associated with girls. As a teenager, Chaz reached the conclusion that he was a lesbian. However, he still wondered why he felt so masculine. Then, as an adult, Bono searched for meaning and contentment in relationships and an unsuccessful music career. In his thirties, he hid from his problems, abusing prescription drugs and becoming reclusive; however, such a lifestyle left him isolated. Bono finally found happiness only by embracing his true identity and transitioning to live openly as a transgender man.

Along the way, there were key relationships that shaped him. There was a constant struggle with his mother, who feared the loss of her child and had concerns about the safety of hormone therapy and surgical procedures. There were girlfriends who struggled to understand and accept Bono's identity. And, sadly, there were the deaths of both the first love of his life and of his father.

In the end, however, Bono overcame all those obstacles when he realized that the only person he needed to please was his true self. He reached a point at which he knew that he must live without fear of how others would perceive him. He could no longer be afraid of the media, his mother, or girlfriends. He could not fear bigots who refused to accept his gender identity and rights as a transgender man. It took bravery for Bono to overcome those fears and become the person he was always meant to be.

Bono provided the world a life lesson through his courage and convictions. He showed one and all that the search for happiness is the most important mission in life and that happiness is the result of being true to one's self. He overcame his personal struggles and reemerged as a successful reality television entertainer, an accomplished author, and an advocate for LGBTQ rights.

CHAPTER 1

A CHILDHOOD IN THE SPOTLIGHT

Four-year-old Chaz Bono was wearing a shiny orange dress, just like his mother. He smiled for everyone watching. His parents loved to show off how cute he was. They were no different than any mom and dad in that way. But this was no dinner party in front of family and friends. Chaz was on stage entertaining hundreds of people in a studio audience—and millions more watching on television. His folks hosted *The Sonny & Cher Comedy Hour*, one of America's top-rated variety shows of the 1970s. Chaz was too young to understand that he was a star. Chaz was also too young to understand his gender identity. Born on March 4, 1969, Chaz was assigned female at birth. Later in life Bono would come to identify as male.

Sonny and Cher perform in a skit for their variety show *The Sonny & Cher Comedy Hour*.

Sonny Bono and Cherilyn Sarkisian (better known as simply Cher) had skyrocketed to stardom in the mid-1960s as the singing duo Sonny and Cher. Their anthem of love and togetherness titled "I Got You, Babe" shot to number one on the charts in the summer of 1965. A number of other hits followed. However, by the time Chaz began appearing on their television show in the early 1970s, the adoration they continued to show for each other publicly was fading in their private life. Their marriage was failing. Chaz was just a child when his parents' divorce became official in 1975.

HIT-MAKING PARENTS

Though Sonny and Cher exploded onto the music scene as a duo, Cher was far more successful as a solo artist. The pair's breakout hit "I Got You, Babe" was their only song that reached number one in the United States, though four other singles soared to the top spot overseas.

Cher, however, became a solo superstar, pumping out hits during her time with Sonny and thereafter, especially in the early 1970s. Her song "Bang, Bang (My Baby Shot Me Down)" (penned by Sonny Bono) reached number two on the Billboard Hot 100 singles chart in 1966. Three further singles—"Gypsies, Tramps & Thieves" (1971), "Half-Breed" (1973), and "Dark Lady" (1974)—all skyrocketed to number one. Each of them was released after Chaz was born.

Cher later had a successful acting career, a high-paying residency in Las Vegas, and a string of hits in the late 1980s. Her biggest smash, however, might have been "Believe." Released in 1998, the song climbed to number one in eight different countries, including the United States.

Like most people, Bono can't recall his days as a toddler. However, old photos and video clips would later tell him the story of a miscast child. Pictures showed a young child dressed in frilly pink dresses and velvet pantsuits, sporting blonde curls as Chaz's adoring parents look on. However, even from a young age, Chaz knew the role wasn't right.

Looking back, Chaz also sees a childhood without roots. His mother moved from one home to another, dragging Chaz along with her. He spent time with his father, too, but because his parents were so busy—in fact, they continued their show together even well after their divorce—Chaz became closer to his nanny, Linda, than either parent. Linda gave Chaz the warmth and attention that all children crave. Chaz received little satisfaction when visiting his father, who was a workaholic. Though he eventually came to embrace his relationship with his dad, Chaz often felt lonely at his house. He spent most of his time there pining for Linda.

SUPPRESSING HIS FEELINGS

Chaz understood at an early age that his parents were celebrities and that work was their first priority. He suppressed his own emotional needs so they wouldn't interfere with his parents' careers. He stayed out of their way and instead developed relationships with his stuffed animals, giving them names and pretending they had feelings. Later in life, Bono realized that he had simply been projecting his own feelings onto his toys. Even through his teenage years and much of his adult life, he suppressed his emotional needs.

What Chaz did realize early in life was that he felt out of place. He preferred wearing clothes and shoes from the boys' section of stores. He

Chaz was a frequent guest alongside his parents on *The Sonny and Cher Comedy Hour*.

was also more interested in play with other boys and the rough-and-tumble games that society often associates with young boys. Chaz didn't relate to girls at his school. Others saw him as a "tomboy."

In his autobiography *Transition* (published in 2011), Bono notes that his aunt, Georganne LaPiere (whom he calls "Aunt Gee"), always associated young Chaz with so-called feminine traits. LaPiere insists that Chaz was soft, gentle, and sweet. While he was too young to remember how he behaved at that age, Bono admits he has spent much time debating with his aunt whether or not her perception of him was true. Bono argues that being sweet and gentle are not necessarily feminine qualities. This distinction is important, as not every girl who is a so-called tomboy and not every "effeminate" boy is transgender. There is not necessarily a correlation between behavior, gender identity, and sexual orientation; each individual has a unique combination of the three. Nonetheless, Bono insists he had a rough-and-tumble side, particularly when he was with his father.

Although Cher admittedly would have preferred Chaz be a little more stereotypically "girly," neither parent expressed strong opposition to his "boyish" behavior. After all, some girls enjoyed dressing in jeans and sneakers and playing sports—fashion and recreation associated more with boys than girls in the 1970s. Chaz was well behaved and respectful of adults. He didn't have trouble making friends. Among his friends was Ricky, with whom he pretended to be a soldier battling in the backyard and played with action figures. Chaz sensed no difference between himself and Ricky or other boys. However, Ricky lived a far more normal life; he was not the child of divorced celebrities.

Soon it became apparent to Chaz that his father was far more accepting of him than his mother. Sonny didn't try to change his clothes, his toys, or his behavior. After Chaz failed to find a keychain with his name on it at his favorite toy store, Uncle Don's, his father suggested he pick out one with a name he liked. Chaz picked "Fred," and Sonny used it as Chaz's nickname thereafter. Although Sonny did not realize his son was transgender, he embraced Chaz's "boyish" interests. They played football in the yard together, and Chaz accompanied his father to the horse races. They watched sports on television. By that time in his life, Chaz was receiving the attention and acceptance from his father that made him content.

CONFLICT WITH MOM

Such was not the case in Chaz's relationship with Cher, who grew increasingly angry about the fashion and activities Chaz embraced. She tried to convince him that he could act like a tomboy while wearing more "feminine" clothes and partaking in so-called girls' activities. After all, as Cher told Chaz, she too had been a tomboy growing up.

The result was a growing conflict and a failed attempt at compromise. Cher allowed Chaz to wear T-shirts and jeans, but only if he wore dresses on more formal occasions. She let him play football but forced him to take ballet lessons as well. She gave him permission to have a birthday party only if a few girls were invited along with Chaz's male friends. Such give-and-take left Chaz feeling like he had lost the battle.

In a roundabout way, the television superhero Wonder Woman helped Chaz finally stand up for himself in second grade. One day, Cher insisted that Chaz wear a jean skirt with Wonder Woman patches on it. That day in school, a boy looked at Chaz in confusion and asked why he was dressing like a girl. Chaz was so angry when he returned home that he confronted his mother and told her he would never again wear a dress. Cher got the message. She never again demanded that Chaz put on a dress.

Cher did not give up, however, in trying to bring out the femininity she wanted to find in her child. In their lavish southern California home, she decorated his room in pink. Chaz, as one might expect, hated it. He again worked up the nerve to make his feelings known to his mother, who redecorated the room more to his liking.

Cher grew increasingly frustrated over her inability to understand her child. Chaz began to believe there was something wrong with his interests, as they took a toll on his relationship with his mother. Cher often ignored him, not just because she was busy entertaining the world but because she didn't know how to relate to him. Chaz was too young to understand that his mother's need to snub him was a direct result of her uneasiness with his gender identity. And because Cher felt uncomfortable with her child, Chaz felt uncomfortable with himself, too. Rather than embrace who he was, he subconsciously rejected it.

Other problems also hindered Chaz's childhood relationship with Cher. Chaz yearned to feel settled. However, after his mother married fellow rock star Gregg Allman, she moved Chaz to a home in Beverly Hills. Then, to a home in

Cher and her second husband, Gregg Allman, are photographed together leaving a Washington, DC, hotel on January 21, 1977.

Malibu. Then, to a home in Westwood. Then, to a home in Santa Monica. Chaz barely got settled in one neighborhood before it seemed like they were planning a move to another. In between moves, they stayed at hotels. Meanwhile, Chaz was also shuttling back and forth for visits with his dad.

Many would consider such a lifestyle glamorous, especially for a child of wealthy celebrities, but Chaz didn't see the constant moves as a fun adventure. They made him uncomfortable. Nonetheless, he was not one to complain. He internalized his frustration. Chaz refused to admit to himself that he hated living like a rich nomad. He couldn't have survived emotionally if he fell apart each time he was forced to move again. After all, he had other issues in his life. One such issue was that, after his stepbrother Elijah was born (when Chaz was seven), his beloved nanny Linda stopped working for the family. His security blanket had disappeared. In her place was a nurse who would take care of Elijah and make life miserable for Chaz.

CHAPTER 2

NEW NANNY, NEW SCHOOLS, NEW PROBLEMS

Perhaps the most fateful and disastrous phone call in Chaz's youth did not include him. The conversation was between his divorced parents. The topic: finding a new nanny for Chaz and his baby half-brother, Elijah.

Cher was in Japan with her second husband, Gregg Allman. She needed somebody to take care of her kids. Sonny suggested a woman named Harriet. Chaz certainly came to regret it; he later described her in his autobiography as having a permanent scowl. But his problems with Harriet extended far beyond disapproving facial expressions.

The welcome arrival of Chaz's younger brother Elijah Blue Allman (pictured here) brought a less desirable figure into the picture for Chaz, a disciplinarian nanny named Harriet.

NANNY TROUBLES

Harriet struggled to handle two-year-old Elijah. However, because he was too young to discipline, she took out her wrath on Chaz. He recalls one night in which she woke him up three times to scream at him. Chaz remembers Harriet dumping the contents of his desk drawer and closet onto his bedroom floor and forcing him to put everything back. She would make up infractions for which to punish him.

Chaz was getting older, but he remained too timid to complain about Harriet to his parents or other adults in his life. On the one occasion that he worked up the courage to tell his mother, she merely instructed him to work things out with Harriet by himself. Chaz became convinced that he would be forced to suffer through what had become a painful relationship.

One might think the logical step for Chaz would have been to move in or at least spend more time with his father. But he took the abuse from Harriet in order to stay with and protect his beloved Elijah, with whom he yearned to spend as much time as possible. Chaz also remained unquestioning of adversity in his life.

REMEMBERING RENÉE RICHARDS

When Chaz was just a child, he was too young to be inspired by one of the first transgender celebrities to fight for trans rights. That was tennis standout Renée Richards.

continued on the next page

Renée Richards plays during the 1977 Women's US Open Tennis Championships.

continued from the previous page

Assigned male at birth, Richards played tennis professionally in men's leagues before transitioning at age forty in 1975. She began to compete in women's tournaments, but soon a journalist revealed that Richards was transgender. Critics complained that the six-foot-two Richards had an unfair advantage over other women and should be banned from tennis. In 1976, the United States Tennis Association (USTA) denied Richards the right to play in the U.S. Open. Richards sued the USTA for discrimination and won. She was then allowed to compete in the U.S. Open. Still, her victory did not go over smoothly with all. Richards received death threats and hate mail. Some players walked off the court rather than compete against her or refused to play her at all. She remained resilient and later reached number twenty in the Women's Tennis Association rankings before retiring in 1981.

Chaz's mother also provided a more exciting time and opened him up to new experiences. Chaz toured with Cher, who performed all over the world. From ages nine to thirteen, he began to realize that he felt more comfortable with adults than he did those his own age. The gay male dancers and female impersonators accepted him, and the feeling was mutual. Chaz developed a kinship with the performers and particularly enjoyed watching the impersonators.

Harriet, however, disapproved of Chaz's relationship with them. As an adult, Bono came to believe that Harriet was homophobic. She had told him that the dancers were "queer" and that rather than concentrating on their performances, they were scanning the audience for potential lovers. She sought to remove Chaz from a lifestyle she disapproved of and tried to convince his parents to place him in a boarding school. It is no wonder he dreaded returning home to Harriet after trips to visit his mother.

TERRIBLE TIME AT SCHOOL

A shrewlike nanny was not Chaz's only childhood problem. As he approached his teenage years, he was placed into Curtis School, which specialized in educating kids struggling with behavioral and emotional issues. Chaz, who was not dealing with such issues, felt traumatized by the experience. He was frightened by students who lost their temper in class. He felt isolated. Chaz became so nervous that he often threw up and was sent to see a child

Chaz Bono stands between his parents at father Bono's restaurant opening in West Hollywood, California, on February 2, 1983.

psychologist. He wondered why he was forced to attend such a school. After all, the only reason he was behind in his education was because he had spent so much time on the road with his mother, not because of any learning disability.

Chaz needed a friend. He found one in Gina, his weekend babysitter's younger sister. Gina was three years older than Chaz. She tagged along with her older sister, who was a welcome visitor whenever Harriet took the day off. Gina and Chaz became so close that they gave each other nicknames. Gina called Chaz "Bones" because it sounded nearly identical to his last name. Chaz called Gina "Beans" because she was skinny like a string bean. Chaz felt more comfortable with Gina than he did with other girls because, as he relates in his autobiography *Transition*, she was "a typical tomboy." The pair spent carefree days together riding bikes and skateboards.

But times were changing by the early 1980s—and so was Chaz's body. Chaz was not prepared emotionally for puberty. His body developed in a way that he didn't like. He was forced to wear a bra, and he hated it. Chaz resented his body's changes. Soon he was getting periods, which terrified him. They were so painful that he spent entire days in bed. A pre-cancerous growth and a large cyst made his periods excruciating.

Life seemed to be turning against Chaz in every respect. Even positives were turned into negatives quickly. A move to Santa Monica resulted in an escape from the school he despised to a Montessori school that fostered openness and creativity. Chaz made friends easily there and even became class president. But when middle school rolled around, the family moved again. Chaz was enrolled in a prep school that he quickly came to hate. He was forced to wear a uniform that included a skirt and blouse. He perceived the female students as conceited and boy-crazy. Chaz didn't fit in with the girls and was teased by the boys. He felt rejected.

The academic requirements of the school did not make matters easier. Chaz had never encountered such a difficult curriculum. He struggled so mightily to keep up that he was forced to work with a tutor several times a week. His grades suffered, as did his confidence. The school offered no other means for him to feel good about himself. It was all about the classroom; there were no theater or music programs in which Chaz could participate.

FOLLOWING MOM CROSS-COUNTRY

That is when fate finally smiled upon him. Years of striving for an acting career had finally paid off for Cher in the early 1980s. She was offered a role in a Broadway play titled *Come Back to the 5 & Dime, Jimmy Dean, Jimmy Dean*. Chaz accompanied his mom to New York for the six-month project. He was ecstatic to learn that Harriet would stay behind.

An incident right before Chaz left for New York had only served to solidify his negative feelings toward Harriet. The nanny had become convinced that Chaz's English teacher was giving him special treatment simply because she had allowed him to make up a test he missed while sick. An extreme

disciplinarian, Harriet called the school princi-
pal and demanded the teacher be fired. Chaz
attempted in vain to explain to Harriet that he
had only received one more day to study than
his fellow classmates. He apologized to his
teacher on behalf of Harriet, who refused to

Cher stands between her *Come Back to the 5 & Dime, Jimmy Dean, Jimmy Dean* cast mates Sandy Dennis and Karen Black backstage on February 19, 1982.

give up the fight. Chaz was then old enough to suspect that his nanny may have been emotionally unbalanced. Chaz was certainly happy to be free of her upon his arrival in New York.

Experiencing life on the opposite side of the country thrilled Chaz. He fell in love with the city known as the Big Apple. He attended Walden School, which promoted freethinking and the arts. He was given the freedom and responsibility to travel from place to place on New York's massive subway system. He took buses and trains to movies and museums or to the park to meet friends or go shopping. Harriet had been his ball and chain. With her no longer hounding him and draining his spirit, Chaz felt more energetic and mature. He even gained the courage to tell his mother about how Harriet had been treating him. One day, he firmly told Cher that if his dreaded nanny was still around when they returned to California, he would move in with his father. Cher certainly took his feelings to heart. Chaz never saw Harriet again.

Not every aspect of the move to New York was a positive one. After all, it was another move in a life with too many of them for Chaz. He yearned desperately to put down roots.

The constant shuffling between visits to his father and mother as well as from one house and school to another took a huge emotional toll on him. Once Chaz got settled in New York, he felt a greater sense of inner peace. Still, he could not shake the sense of being a nomad.

That feeling helped overshadow another one for Chaz: his growing discomfort with his identity. He began to feel like there was something physically wrong with him. The abuse he was forced to endure from Harriet had worsened those feelings. He realized there was a disconnect between his body and mind. He had yet to identify the issue, but his anxiety could not be ignored. Chaz was on the verge of taking an important step in his journey through life.

CHAPTER 3

BIG CHANGES IN THE BIG APPLE

Chaz was watching a movie when a light went off. Not literally—it was the light in Chaz's head. He and Gina, who had flown to New York from California to help celebrate his thirteenth birthday, were watching a film called *Personal Best.* In a scene where two women began kissing in the movie, Chaz felt something stir inside of him. He says that's the moment when he realized that he, too, was attracted to women. At that point, Chaz did not yet identify as transgender; however, he did identify as a lesbian. (It is worth noting that there is no direct correlation between sexual orientation—the sex to which an individual is attracted—and gender identity.)

FIRST STEPS TO FINDING HIMSELF

After his realization that he was attracted to women, a cloud of doubt dissipated for Chaz. He was beginning to understand why he felt so uncomfortable with expectations others seemed to have for him. He also began to associate his "tomboyish" behavior that teachers, his nanny, and his own mother had tried to suppress for so many years with his attraction to women. After all, he has always hated his mother's attempts to make him conform to her own stereotypically feminine idea of how Chaz should dress. Chaz even associated his desire to hang out with boys rather than girls as a youth to his sexual orientation. Aspects of his childhood that had long troubled him now began to make sense. Like any teenager, Chaz was trying to find himself.

Later in life, Chaz would no longer identify as a lesbian but, rather, as a straight transgender man. However, at the time, his discovery answered many questions. More important, it boosted his confidence in his own identity. After six months in New York, Chaz returned to Los Angeles with his newfound identity. He was back at Curtis School, which now had fewer students. That meant less of an opportunity to find new companions. As a result, Gina remained Chaz's only friend. Chaz came out to Gina as a lesbian. He was relieved that Gina was unfazed by the news. They had so much in common and were such close friends that Chaz's revelation did not affect their friendship. Gina was straight but completely supportive of Chaz's orientation; she didn't care that Chaz was a lesbian.

Chaz, however, did care that Gina was straight. While Gina was a supportive friend, Chaz had no friends who also identified as lesbians. Homosexuality was not as widely accepted in the early 1980s as it has become in the decades since. Chaz could hang out with gay men who worked in his mother's shows, but he had no other role models in the LGBTQ world. There were few gay characters on television. Chaz knew about gay bars where lesbians mingled, but he also knew he couldn't get into such establishments as an underage teenager.

That same year, close to Christmas, Chaz and a group of his mother's friends had gathered in her bedroom to watch a television special in which Cher was featured. Chaz was sitting on the floor when he was struck by the beauty of a woman who entered. Her name was Joan Stephens. He had met her previously, but his more developed awareness of his sexual attraction to women gave him a different view this time. Joan also identified as a lesbian.

It could best be described as a crush. After all, Chaz was still just thirteen. Joan, however, was thirty-five at the time. Chaz realized that their differences in age precluded him from forging a romantic relationship with Joan, but he did benefit from her wisdom and experiences as the first adult lesbian in his life. She provided advice that strengthened the sense in him that all would turn out well. Joan, who met societal standards to be considered quite feminine, dated the rather "masculine" women with whom Chaz closely identified. He yearned at the time to be just like the women Joan dated. It was the beginning of a close relationship with Joan, one that would grow and last for more than a decade.

ACTING SCHOOL

A birthday gift from his mother opened up another new path for Chaz—one that could lead a potential acting career. Cher enrolled Chaz in the Lee Strasberg Theater & Film Institute for the summer. His initial displeasure at spending his weekends taking acting classes

A photograph and a statue of Lee Strasberg are prominently displayed inside the Lee Strasberg Theater and Film Institute in West Hollywood, California.

was gradually replaced with a genuine enthusiasm. He not only learned a craft, but he made new friends with a passion for creativity that he shared. He even branched out into singing and dancing.

Chaz also kissed a girl for the first time at an end-of-semester party. He landed his first job, toiling as a busboy at a new Italian restaurant opened by his father, with whom he spent more time and grew closer. His ability to make money on his own strengthened his self-image. It was a summer he would never forget.

The experiences at Lee Strasberg stirred up a yearning in Chaz to move back to New York and attend the Fiorello H. LaGuardia High School of Music & Art and Performing Arts. After badgering his mother about it constantly, she scheduled an audition for him. She was quite concerned given her awareness that the vast majority of kids who try out for LaGuardia don't make the cut. She didn't want Chaz to be emotionally scarred by rejection. However, he worked diligently all summer, rehearsing the two monologues that he was to perform at the audition.

Chaz was ready. He performed the monologues well enough to pass the first test. Then, he would have to read another monologue in front of a panel of seniors and teachers, as well as the head of the drama department. He also needed to perform well enough in improvisations with other potential students to be accepted into the school. When Chaz had finished, he had no idea whether or not he would be accepted. He waited nervously in his hotel room.

Chaz attended the renowned Fiorello H. LaGuardia High School of Music & Art and Performing Arts for high school.

BIG THUMBS-UP

The phone rang. It was Tony Abeson, an acting teacher from LaGuardia High School with an unusual sense of humor. "In the midst of our confusion," he told the nervous teenager, "we've decided to accept you." Chaz was so delighted

ONE HECK OF AN ALUMNI LIST

New York City's Fiorello H. LaGuardia High School of Music & Art and Performing Arts, often known as simply LaGuardia, has produced some of the most famous and successful entertainers in the United States since it first opened in 1961. Besides Chaz Bono, other notable alumni of LaGuardia include actor Jennifer Aniston, who gained fame for her role in the hit 1990s television sitcom *Friends*, actor and singer Liza Minnelli, and popular rapper Nicki Minaj. Other actors—such as Al Pacino, Wesley Snipes, and Robert De Niro—attended the school for a portion of their education, ultimately transferring elsewhere or dropping out to pursue acting full time. The high school became a fixture of popular culture thanks to the 1980 musical film *Fame*, based on the school, and the subsequent television series based on the film, which ran from 1982 until 1987.

he began jumping up and down on his bed. A week later, he was officially a student at LaGuardia. Rumors surfaced that he was accepted only because he was the child of the famous Sonny and Cher, but they soon dissipated.

Not all was well, however. Since Cher was busily trying to further her own acting career in Los Angeles, she did not move to New York with

Pictured is Anna Strasberg, the widow of Lee Strasberg and caretaker of Chaz while he attended high school in New York.

Chaz. He was forced to live with Anna Strasberg, the widow of Lee and a good friend of Cher's. Chaz liked Anna and her two sons but did not appreciate her pushing him to become what she perceived as more feminine. She strongly encouraged him to grow his hair longer and dress more like a young woman.

Chaz often called Joan for encouragement. She simply told Chaz to be himself and not get discouraged. Later in life, Bono became aware that many transgender and gender non-conforming youth are too often told by parents and other adults that there is something wrong with the way they dress or behave. Reassurance from Joan gave Chaz a belief that, by just being himself, he was truly on the right path.

LaGuardia High School provided a positive experience. He forged new friendships and gained a sense of community with his fellow classmates. Chaz was open about his identity as a lesbian, and his classmates accepted him. Such acceptance was welcome after years of being unsure how to fit in. Chaz was also thrilled to be in an institution that gave him a creative outlet and focused less on academics—an area where he hadn't always excelled. He was perfectly satisfied to receive fair grades, so long as he could develop his acting and be accepted among his peers.

Cher moved back to New York during Chaz's junior year of high school. Though he enjoyed their time together, she remained critical of his fashion choices and lack of femininity. Chaz realized that he would soon have to tell his mother that he identified as a lesbian. He had already told his grandmother and aunt, both of whom proved accepting. However, neither had shared Chaz's revelation with Cher. The whole family believed that she would be horrified. And because Cher was so busy, it had been easy to keep it a secret from her.

After his mother caught Chaz cuddling on the couch with a girl, she said nothing. However, Chaz sensed a change in his mother after the incident. She seemed distant. In fact, she did not even attend his seventeenth birthday party. Chaz suspected that his mother was more upset about his perceived masculinity than judgmental that he identified as a lesbian. At that point, Chaz did not yet identify as a transgender man. Chaz was trying to figure out the best way to be open and come out to his parents as a lesbian. It wouldn't be long before he would work up the courage to do just that.

CHAPTER 4

COMING OUT TO MOM AND THE WORLD

Chaz was enjoying a bike ride one pleasant June day after his junior year of high school when he pedaled into a parade. However, this wasn't any ordinary parade; it happened to be the annual New York City Pride March—an annual gay pride parade. Chaz was thrilled.

He rode alongside and felt a sense of kinship with other members of the LGBTQ community. Since coming out, he had always known that he wasn't alone, but he understood now that there was an entire movement of people proud of their identity and fighting to protect the rights of their community at large—including teenagers like Chaz. It was an actual political movement with brave leaders working to gain

Protestors march during the Gay and Lesbian Pride March in New York City, NY, on June 26, 1988.

societal acceptance. That day, Chaz saw folks marching for various gay organizations. The experience made Chaz proud and happy to identify as a lesbian.

EXPLORING HIS ATTRACTION

Stumbling upon a pride parade and being immersed in New York culture helped solidify Chaz's identity as a lesbian, and the environment certainly made him feel like he finally fit in. There was something holding him back, however, from fully embracing lesbian subculture. The hesitation came from others who asked him a fairly common question that gay and lesbian youth face: How did he know he was a lesbian if he had yet to make love to a man? Chaz knew deep down that it would not change his attraction toward women, but he indeed pushed himself into a sexual encounter with a heterosexual man whom he knew. It proved to be a passionless event.

Other dates with men cemented his belief that he was not interested in them. Chaz occasionally dressed up in what he felt were more feminine outfits in an attempt to attract men who seemed cool or handsome. Though later in life, he came to realize that his willingness to experiment revealed that he was not wholly comfortable identifying as a lesbian either. Any physical attraction that Chaz felt for a man was based on his desire to express his male gender, although at the time, a teenage Chaz didn't fully grasp this desire or know how to express it. Still, he could later point to ways in which he began to identify his gender identity. As an actor, for instance, he felt ill suited to play the roles of women. But when he played a male character in a production of Shakespeare's *A Midsummer Night's Dream*, he nailed it.

Early in his freshman year as a student at New York University's film school, Bono decided that he was ready to come out of the closet to his father. Sonny, suspecting that his child may identify as a lesbian, gave Chaz an opening by asking during a visit if there was anything Chaz wanted to tell him. Chaz confirmed Sonny's suspicions and explained to his father that he had been afraid the revelation would create tension in their relationship. However, Sonny expressed his unconditional love for Chaz.

SHARING WITH CHER

Chaz knew, however, that the same would not be true of his mother. It should have been easy to keep his identity a secret, despite a developing relationship with a young woman named Heidi. After all, he was living in New York and Cher was in Los Angeles. However, Sonny decided to spill the beans. When Cher called Chaz to discuss it, she was furious. Not only had she learned from her ex-husband that her child identified as a lesbian, but she was enraged to know that Chaz had kept it a secret from her for so long. Chaz insisted that being open and honest about his sexual orientation would bring him and his mother closer, but Cher insisted that it would pull them further apart. Not only that, but she asked Chaz to move out of her New York apartment.

Cher had calmed down a week later, when she asked Chaz to fly to Los Angeles with his girlfriend Heidi to talk. Chaz was relieved that his mother finally knew, but he was afraid of a confrontation. Cher expressed far greater understanding, explaining that she had been mostly upset about having to hear the news from Sonny rather than from her own child. Yet, Chaz still sensed a genuine disappointment from his mother that her precious offspring identified as a lesbian. He was happy, however, that Cher was working to adjust. She indeed became more accepting with time.

Bono later wrote about the experience in his book *Family Outing* (1998). He realized by then the importance of coming out on one's own terms rather than having someone else push a gay or lesbian person out of the closet. He expressed that openness is a key to convincing others to be comfortable with their sexual orientation and gender identity.

"The people that have been outed are not necessarily the ones that come out as role models," Bono told television news network CNN in an interview that year. "I think what we've seen is that when someone is outed...it makes them

Chaz performs in Woodland Hills, California, on November 13, 1993.

retreat to the closet for a time. I think as a community we've seen what the difference is and the value in people who make the decision to come out on their own because they don't want to be hiding anymore."

Coming out to his parents brought Bono great relief. His newfound openness with his parents gave him the confidence to move in with Heidi, with whom he had fallen deeply in love, with no worries about their reaction. Heidi Shink was an accomplished musician who taught him how to play piano and guitar. Bono also discovered through her that he boasted a strong singing voice, just like his parents. However, Shink also placed pressure on Bono to abandon what she felt was too masculine a style of hair and dress.

Bono went along, and later in life he admitted that his compliance showed a lack of self-awareness. He so needed love and acceptance from Shink that he let her control him. It would not be the first time he downplayed his masculinity for fear of losing a woman. In fact, Bono even dropped out of college for Shink—though it was not a difficult decision for him, and it caused no stress in the family. She was moving on after graduation, and he did not want to risk losing her. He was skeptical about the importance of higher education in his life anyway.

Since nobody else in his family aside from his aunt had attended college, not a peep of protest was raised.

A NEW DIRECTION

But what was Bono to do now? The end of his college education meant the beginning of a new career. During a trip to Europe with Shink, he expressed what had been on his mind for a while. He wanted to start a rock band with her. He had gained confidence as a musician and songwriter. He also had no other realistic career ambitions. He was passionately in love with Shink, who was passionately in love with music. It all fit together, and she embraced his plan.

They bought such essentials as a guitar, a drum set, and a keyboard, and the couple set out to write and play music. Cher arranged for them to work with singer and guitar player Bob Weir, one of the founding members of the legendary band the Grateful Dead. Weir invited the fledgling musicians to his house to record a demo. Bono admitted that the music was awful, but Weir encouraged them to continue. They found a drummer, bass player, guitarist, and keyboardist, and they practiced for a year to strengthen their sound. The group spent virtually every moment together.

Bono and his bandmates performed well enough in the studio to land a meeting with representatives for Geffen Records, which paid them and hired a mentor to work on their style while scheduling gigs in New York. All was well. However, Bono felt uncomfortable with the stereotypically feminine costumes—something that

Bono and his Ceremony band mate Chance (Heidi Shink) pose with their guitars during a promotional performance in London, England, in 1993.

COMING OUT TO MOM AND THE WORLD

the label and his bandmates felt were important. He became painfully aware that he was donning clothes that felt far more feminine than anything else he had worn in his life.

Bono also felt that he needed to hide his sexual orientation from the public. He heard that a tabloid was about to expose him as a lesbian, which he feared would wreck the music deal. Geffen did not drop the band after the story was published, but Bono and Shink were forced to hide that they were a couple. It was believed at the time that openly gay and lesbian musicians could not succeed. Bono, whose gender expression was still perceived as female, pretended instead that he was dating his male guitar player.

Bono learned that the tabloids had been waiting for him to become a public figure beyond his association with Sonny and Cher so they could expose his sexual orientation. Meanwhile, the LGBTQ community criticized him for not coming out of the closet publicly. Fearful of the professional repercussions, Bono denied that he identified as a lesbian for the next three years. He felt like he was living a lie, and he hated himself for it.

The music business soon became a grind for Bono. The joy with which it began eventually drained away. The band, which performed under the name Ceremony, produced one album in 1993 titled *Hang Out Your Poetry*. It received a merely lukewarm response.

The strain of trying to succeed while keeping their relationship secret had been wreaking

BIG NIGHT FOR THE BAND

The rock band Ceremony struggled to make a name for itself, but it did enjoy one memorable night during a live performance in Flint, Michigan, in 1993. The group had been booked to play in a Halloween show sponsored by a local radio station. Bono and his fellow band members had gained little success, so they weren't expecting much of a reaction from the audience.

However, when the guitarist began playing the opening riff from their song "Could've Been Love," the fans went wild. The band members turned around to see if somebody famous had come on stage behind them, but they soon realized that the shocking and wonderful reaction was for their song, which had become a local hit in Flint. It marked the first and last time Ceremony felt so appreciated on stage, but Bono would never forget it. He had gotten a feel, though for just a short time, for what it's like to be a rock star.

havoc on Bono and Shink for quite some time before *Hang Out Your Poetry* was released. They had been living in Los Angeles, where they found too many distractions. Bono was crushed when Shink explained that she wanted to date other people. He then fell out of love with her and into the arms of his longtime, older crush Joan Stephens. He had been too young to court Stephens when they first met. But not anymore. Bono and Stephens began a relationship.

It was a relationship unlike any other he had experienced. Stephens treated him like he yearned to be treated—as a man. He had not yet come to identify as transgender. However, Joan embraced his masculinity, helping Bono come to terms with his gender identity and expression.

CHAPTER 5

YEARS OF GROWTH AND ACTIVISM

Though Ceremony never found its path to becoming a successful rock band, it did receive some notoriety. That meant interviews with the media, something Bono dreaded.

He had to dress like a woman. He had to wear his hair in a feminine style. He had to wear makeup. He had to pretend to identify as heterosexual. He had to play make-believe with the media. For five years, Bono had toiled to forge a career that he was no longer enjoying. He was no closer to figuring out what he wanted to do professionally.

Bono was now twenty-four years old and living two different lives: a sad, repressed one as a musician and a happy, more authentic one with Joan. He had fallen passionately in love with the older woman. He found the courage to tell his mother about the relationship, and to his delight, she embraced the news.

LOSING THE LOVE OF HIS LIFE

Bono had at last found a sliver of joy in his personal life, but that, too, soon came crashing down. Stephens was diagnosed with non-Hodgkin lymphoma, an aggressive cancer that had moved to her bones. The timing coincided with a three-week tour to promote the release of one of Ceremony's singles. Bono would have greatly preferred to remain by Stephens's side. He felt relieved when doctors assured him that 95 percent of patients suffering from the same cancer experience remission.

Chemotherapy indeed relieved Stephens's symptoms, but she would never fully recover. The pattern had begun. Stephens would fall sick, receive treatments, feel better, and then get sick again. But the periods of relative health grew shorter. Not only did Bono watch Stephens's developments with alarm, but he also became discouraged when not one radio station to which Ceremony promoted its single added the song to its playlist.

Doctors finally decided on one more round of chemotherapy for Joan. If that did not work, they would let the cancer run its course. Bono was devastated. He was so distraught that he began to take Stephens's prescription drug Percodan to relieve his anxiety. It was his first step to an addiction that nearly destroyed his life as well. Joan Stephens died on February 4, 1994, just a month before Bono turned twenty-five.

Bono could not grieve the loss of Stephens unattached. He was too vulnerable and scared to be alone. He soon met a woman named Tracy, an alcoholic who was still in love with her ex-girlfriend. Further bad news ensued. Ceremony was dropped from their record label, ending Bono's music career. He was forced to take a job as a bartender at a lesbian club in Los Angeles to make ends meet. He was so terrible at it that he decided to quit. Meanwhile, his abuse of Stephens's painkiller prescription was leading to an addiction.

BONO THE WRITER

Though his drug problem would eventually worsen, fate at least gave Bono a purpose. The *Advocate*, a magazine that promotes gay rights and addresses topics of interest to the LGBTQ community, asked Bono to pen an article about coming out of the closet as a lesbian. While he pondered that offer, he asked the editor-in-chief of the *Advocate* for a job as a writer. In February 1995, Bono announced to the world that he identified as a lesbian. He was soon contacted by a variety of gay rights organizations asking him to become involved with their work.

A year later, Bono was working with the Human Rights Campaign as its National Coming Out Project spokesperson. He never fully realized the extent to which the LGBTQ community had been discriminated against legally. He passionately spoke out for his and his community's civil rights. He embraced the opportunity to help those facing similar struggles to his own. In this context he wrote *Family Outing*, his 1998 book that served as a guide for young LGBTQ-identifying persons to come out to their parents. Bono soon accepted a full-time job at a fine salary with the Gay and Lesbian Alliance Against Defamation (GLAAD).

His professional life was thriving, but his personal life was a mess. Bono remained distraught over the loss of Joan. He became dependent

CEO and president of GLAAD Sarah Kate Ellis speaks at the 26th Annual GLAAD Media Awards on March 21, 2015. In the late 1990s, Chaz Bono worked for the organization to advance LGBTQ rights.

on the prescription painkiller Vicodin to ease his emotional pain—a dangerous abuse of the drug's intended use. Around the same time, Bono grew angry with his father, who was now a Republican congressman for the state of California. Sonny Bono cosponsored the Defense of Marriage Act (1996), which defined marriage for federal purposes as being between a man and woman.

Bono, however, learned a lesson about holding grudges when his father died in a skiing accident in January 1998. He regretted not having come to terms with his dad, with whom he cherished a loving and accepting relationship throughout most of his life. He issued a statement to the media at the time of his father's death admitting that he and his father differed on some political issues but that Sonny had been very supportive of his personal life and career.

By that point, Bono was using painkillers daily. He was also fired from GLAAD after making a comment to a newspaper that the TV sitcom *Ellen*, whose star Ellen DeGeneres had recently come out of the closet, had become too focused on gay and lesbian issues for a national audience. Bono felt his comment had been taken out of context, but the LGBTQ community shunned Bono after it received widespread attention. He tried to defend himself, but to no avail. He was out of a job.

Sonny Bono was a U.S. representative for the state of California from 1995 until his tragic death in 1998.

DESPERATE TIMES

Bono spent more time at home, where he continued to abuse Vicodin so heavily that he went into liver failure at the age of thirty. He grew so

THE IMPACT OF *ELLEN*

As part of his job with the Gay and Lesbian Alliance Against Defamation, Bono spent a great deal of time working with comedian Ellen DeGeneres, whose sitcom *Ellen* was a hit series from 1994 to 1998.

The show, however, received falling ratings every year it was on the air from 1994 to 1998. The announcement by DeGeneres in 1997 that she was a lesbian did not attract viewers. In fact, the ratings continued to plummet thereafter, and the show was cancelled in 1998.

DeGeneres, however, bounced back when she launched her own afternoon talk show in 2003. It has since remained a highly popular program. DeGeneres has since become an iconic figure in the entertainment industry, continuing to defend LGBTQ rights, host major award shows, and score major film roles.

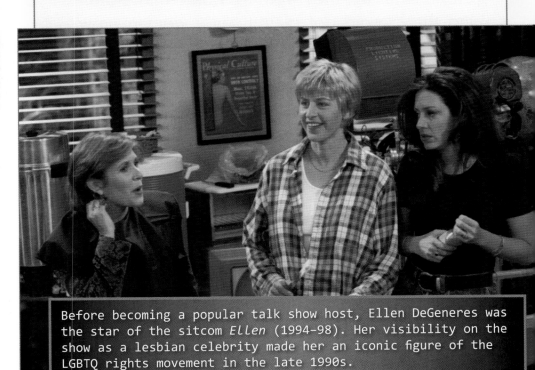

Before becoming a popular talk show host, Ellen DeGeneres was the star of the sitcom *Ellen* (1994-98). Her visibility on the show as a lesbian celebrity made her an iconic figure of the LGBTQ rights movement in the late 1990s.

depressed that he considered checking himself into a mental hospital. His entire existence came to revolve around his next drug fix.

His ex-girlfriend and former bandmate Heidi Shink soon came to the rescue. She returned to Bono's life to advise him to check into rehab. He not only did that, but he also met a new girlfriend, a woman named Kathy, at a recovery support group meeting. She proved to be a role model in Bono's attempt to stay sober. Soon she accepted an invitation to move in with him. She was a social butterfly, which helped Bono meet new people and come out of his drug haze.

The more Bono hung out with lesbians, however, the less he felt he had in common with them. After all, they were all women. The feeling that he did not identify as a woman grew stronger the more he compared himself to his friends. He did not yet identify as a transgender man, but he knew he was not comfortable with his identity as a "butch," or more masculine, lesbian. He perceived such an admission as a sign of desperation. He feared how others would view him. He loathed his gender expression, but was not sure if he wanted to take the steps toward transitioning.

That period of uncertainty was about to

end. Bono began to speak openly with his partner Kathy about transitioning. She was uncomfortable with the topic and then hostile toward Bono. However, he could not deny his identity—as much as he tried. He would later reveal that, at the time, he listed dozens of reasons to hide his gender identity as a man. They included the potential loss of Kathy, the risk that his mother would disown him, the reaction of the media, the increased risks of physical assault and discrimination, the possible consequences of any medical or surgical intervention to affirm his gender expression, and the effect a transition might have on his social life.

In late 2001, Bono was given prescription painkillers following a surgical procedure. That led to a relapse back into addiction. He broke up with Kathy and rarely left his home. At his mother's request, he saw a therapist and continued to go to his support group. However, Bono simply pretended to be sober. He watched television and played video games constantly. He had been smoking cigarettes since he was a teenager, but he now increased his cigarette use to two or three packs a day. His life revolved around drugs.

Chaz hit rock bottom at age thirty-four.

It was January 2004 when he expressed to his therapist the futility of seeing her. He told her he simply wanted to take drugs and be left alone. He late recalled the conversation in his 2011 autobiography, *Transition*. According to Bono, his therapist posited, "So you want to slowly kill yourself and destroy all the relationships in your life?" Bono replied that he did; he felt no shame in admitting it. However, the exchange gave him a sense of clarity that grew. He realized that he did not truly want to die. Two months later, he checked into a drug rehabilitation treatment facility in Arizona. He had taken the first step to turning his life around.

CHAPTER 6

GETTING SOBER, FINDING IDENTITY

Chaz Bono was scared to do what he knew he had to do—that is, get off drugs. At the peak of his addiction, he was taking ten doses of the painkiller oxycodone every day. He even took one the morning he checked into rehab to try to avoid the withdrawal.

Bono's fear of withdrawal was justified. He had been a drug addict for a decade at that point and could not have fully braced himself for the painful process of no longer feeding his addiction. He felt like he was dying during the course of five agonizing days of withdrawal at his rehab facility. But when the withdrawals ended and the rehabilitation began, Bono felt a sense of freedom and clarity. He started socializing with others. He made friends. He laughed. He was enjoying life again. So positive was his experience that after his release from rehab, he did four months of outpatient treatment to ensure he remained clean.

After rehab, Bono also began speaking with counsellors about starting his transition. Rather than trying to talk him out of it, they supported his desire to begin living openly as a transgender man. His therapist suggested he maintain his sobriety for one year before taking steps toward his transition from a female to male.

Bono was not about to make the same mistake twice with his mother. He still regretted not informing her first when he came to identify as a lesbian, so he worked up the courage to tell her about his gender identity. Cher stunned him by suggesting that he begin his transition immediately. Though she feared any possible health risks, Bono felt relieved about her support.

Coming out as transgender to others in his life would not be easy. Bono met a lesbian named Robin at a Halloween party that year. They began a relationship, but she expressed disappointment when he explained to her that he was a trans man. At that point, Bono was not ready to tell a woman "love me as a transgender man or leave me." Instead, he lied and told Robin that he remained unsure about transitioning. The two would eventually break up for unrelated reasons, but it raised the consideration that as a heterosexual man, Bono might no longer be able to date lesbian-identifying women.

Bono was fearful over how he would be perceived by others after coming out, so he chose at the time to put off any medical or surgical steps of his transition. Instead, he would alter other aspects of his gender expression, dressing and behaving in a way he felt was more masculine. He even stopped seeing the therapist who had been preparing him for his transition from female to male.

A NEW WOMAN AND A NEW DIRECTION

Loneliness once again set in for Bono when his beloved cat, Stinky, died in March 2005. However, just five months later, a new friend would enter his life that would not only provide companionship but also ease him forward into reassuming his transition from female to male. Her name was Jennifer (or simply Jenny) Elia, and she, too, was a recovering addict. Though

Bono sought to take their relationship more slowly that he had with women in the past, the two became inseparable.

Elia was accepting of Bono's male gender expression. Unlike previous girlfriends, she never tried to draw out a "feminine" side that didn't exist. When Bono finally expressed his gender identity to Elia and that he was considering a transition, she appeared too surprised to react. But the admission awakened Bono to the fact that he, indeed, had not lost his desire to transition. Part of him had feared that any medical steps of a transition would ruin his identity. He now realized that being male was always his true identity; any steps to reaffirm his gender expression could only help others understand his identity—not ruin it.

Bono finally understood that only fear had held him back from transitioning. When reevaluating his dormant career—he had not made any significant income since 2002—he did not even yearn to return to his activism work for the lesbian community. After all, once he identified as a transgender man, Bono no longer identified as a lesbian; he was a heterosexual man.

His first job after recovering from his drug addiction came courtesy of reality television. He was asked by VHI to participate in a show called *Celebrity Fit Club*, which features a weight-loss competition. Bono not only needed the money, but he sensed that he would feel more confident about transitioning if he lost fat and gained muscle first. However, Bono's experience on the show proved disappointing because he was not taught how to lose weight. The producers encouraged significant weight loss without adding muscle for drastic—but short-term—results. Bono dropped twenty-five pounds at the expense of being hungry and irritable all day.

Bono then tried to springboard from his appearance on *Celebrity Fit Club* into more TV opportunities, but to no avail. He cowrote a made-for-television movie script about two female friends—one lesbian and one heterosexual—but it was rejected. Frustrated and depressed, Bono spent most of his time at home playing video games. His life had come to a standstill. He realized that only one action would push it back in the right direction. He needed to follow through with his transition from female to male.

Other factors weighed into his decision, too. A combination of his weight and aspects of his body that he did not feel matched his gender identity also motivated Bono to seek surgical intervention to reaffirm his gender

Bono was inspired in part by a Barbara Walters interview with transgender kids. Here, Walters stands at a Broadway premiere in New York City, New York, on March 23, 2000.

expression. At the age of thirty-eight, Bono decided to have his breasts removed.

Bono needed inspiration to take further steps in his transition. Such inspiration came from a television program in which famed newscaster Barbara Walters interviewed transgender youth. Bono did not believe the program would affect him because its subjects were children, not adults like him. But when his partner Jenny asked him if he had felt the same way as a child as those featured on the program did, he admitted that he had. He became determined to follow through further with his transition.

GREAT ROLE MODEL

Soon thereafter, Bono met a transgender man named Luke whom he had known before Luke's transition from female to male. Bono was not nearly as impressed with the physical changes in Luke's gender expression as he was with what he detected emotionally. Luke exuded joyful contentment. Bono finally realized that transition was inevitable if he ever wanted to be as happy as Luke. Although he also remained aware that as a minor celebrity and the offspring of legendary entertainers,

THE STORY OF CHRISTINE JORGENSEN

It took a great deal of courage for Chaz Bono to transition from female to male in 2009, so one can only imagine how much courage it took Christine Jorgensen, an American soldier who fought in World War II, to transition from male to female in the early 1950s.

Jorgensen learned about surgical procedures to reaffirm gender expression after her time in the U.S. Army. In 1951, she traveled to Denmark (the transition

Christine Jorgensen speaks to reporters at John F. Kennedy International Airport (then known as Idlewild Airport) in Queens, New York, on February 12, 1953.

procedures were not available at the time in the United States) to undergo a series of operations and hormone treatments as part of her transition. She was the first widely known American transgender individual to undergo gender reassignment surgeries.

In early 1953, Jorgensen moved back from Denmark to the United States. She then launched a career as an entertainer and an advocate for transgender rights. Her transition from male to female challenged American perceptions of gender and sex. She was a true pioneer.

the media would likely follow his transition closely and report on it.

All the fears resurfaced. Would Jenny leave him? Would he be snubbed by his family and friends? Would the lesbian community view him as a traitor? Would his professional life be doomed? In January 2008, Bono wrote a letter to himself that expressed the perceived positives and negatives of transitioning. He later published the letter in *Transition*. In the letter, Bono criticized himself for having hidden his gender identity, but he also wrote about the need to conquer his fear of transitioning.

Bono started to feel out how other people in his life would react, but knew that it was a decision he had to make on his own. He could not allow other to make what would be the biggest decision of his life for him. After all, Elia had already assured him once before that she would stay by his side but then later told him she didn't know if she could accept such a change in him.

Bono also worried about how his mother would take the news. After all, the media pressure on her if he transitioned would be overwhelming. His therapist reminded him that he was powerless over others. His first obligation was to himself. Those were the words Bono had to hear. He had never put his own feelings ahead of those of others, but he needed to learn to do just that if he wanted to be happy.

It was not easy for Bono to stand up to his partner Jenny, who reacted with anger when he told her his plans. She called him selfish for thinking only of himself. She also asserted that Bono would not be happier or any more confident if he transitioned. She threatened that the stress of the transition would cause her to go back on drugs. But Bono not only stood his ground, he flew into a rage. He yelled at Elia that he was a man. Rather than let out any of the anger he was feeling, Bono left the house and drove away.

Chaz Bono stands outside the Outfest 2005 Awards Night on July 17, 2005.

Elia, who was taken aback by the show of temper, agreed to accompany Bono to couples therapy. She gradually became more accepting of his decision. Bono also received support from his doctor, who spoke about hormone therapy and the need for her patient to lose more weight through a healthier diet. Bono feared his toughest hurdle would be acceptance from his mother, but she surprised him by claiming to be fine with the transition. Though he understood now that his own feelings must come before those of anyone else, he still wanted his mother's acceptance. Once he had that support, it was full speed ahead. Chaz Bono was ready to complete his transition.

CHAPTER 7

BECOMING AN ADVOCATE

Christmas is a festive time when many families come together, but Chaz Bono and his mother, Cher, were in no mood to sing "Jingle Bells" when they met in Malibu, California, for Christmas 2008. Bono sensed tension between them that hadn't been evident in July, when he first revealed his plans to transition.

The best friend of his half-brother, Elijah, flat-out asked Bono about his New Year's plans and if he was going to transition. Bono answered in the affirmative and cast a glance at Cher, who appeared scared. She had obviously told the family and had just as obviously grown uncomfortable with Bono's transition. However, Bono was no longer controlled by fear. He was going full-steam ahead, making arrangements to begin steps of his transition on March 20, 2009, two weeks after his fortieth birthday.

BEGINNING HORMONE THERAPY

Cher had at first expressed a desire to meet with him, as well as his therapist and doctor, but Bono did not hear from her for months. He was pleased that other family members voiced their approval, but the feelings of others no longer factored in. Chaz's own feelings were all that mattered now.

Bono shed all his doubts when he visited the doctor in late winter 2009. He began using a prescription for AndroGel, a topical gel that raises the levels of testosterone in the body. He had experienced no changes after a couple weeks, so he returned to the doctor. This time Cher came too—and she was not happy that Bono had started his transition. She assumed he would wait several years. She also feared a negative reaction from her friends and the media would affect her career.

Cher asked her son if his career ambition now was to be a transgender advocate. He replied that he indeed hoped to work with

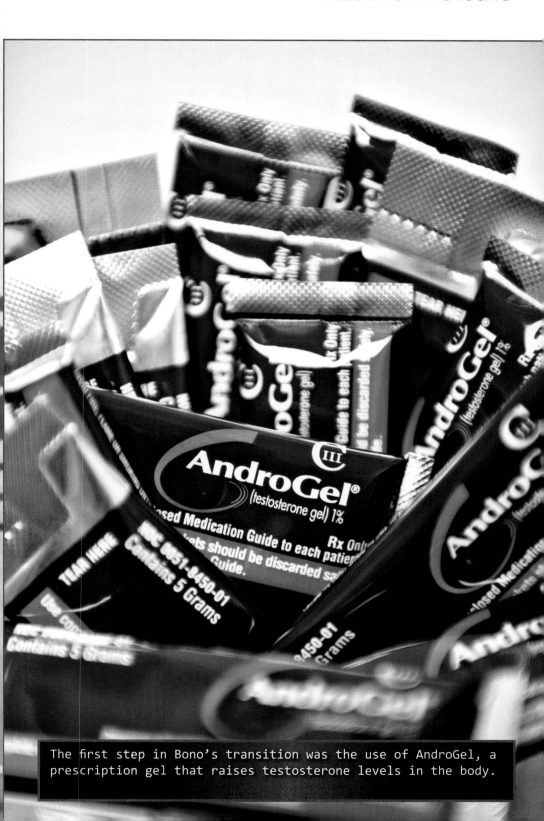

The first step in Bono's transition was the use of AndroGel, a prescription gel that raises testosterone levels in the body.

the transgender community, just as he had previously worked as an advocate for gay and lesbian rights. Cher expressed dread that her son would be the target of public ridicule. Bono knew that his transition might create a media circus, but he believed that if he spoke about how he came to embrace his new identity, others would embrace him for his courage and self-awareness. He feared nothing.

Meanwhile, the hormones were beginning to work, and Bono felt more energetic and focused than ever. He decided to return to school and get his degree. He thought about becoming a therapist who could help other members of the LGBTQ community or a professor of gender and sexuality studies. He was soon accepted into Antioch College in Yellow Springs, Ohio.

Bono's body started to change in response to the AndroGel. He felt stronger. His sex drive increased. He became more muscular. The hair on his legs thickened and darkened. Hair appeared on his navel and eventually spread to his chest. He also experienced acne on his face and upper body, but he had to take the bad with the good. And the good was certainly outweighing the bad. He was happy. He

During his transition, Bono decided to go back to school at Antioch College to study gender and sexuality.

felt comfortable in his body for the first time in his life.

COMING OUT AGAIN

Bono hoped to remain private about his transition for a few months, but soon the gossip television show *TMZ* and the gossip magazine *National Enquirer* learned about it. One day, publicist Howard Bragman told Bono that *TMZ* was about to announce the transition on national television in just thirty minutes. Bono sat frozen, but he also felt a sense of relief that it would all be over soon. He released a statement for the media through Bragman that became national news on June 11, 2009. It read:

> *Chaz, after many years of consideration, has made the courageous decision to honor his true identity. He is proud of his decision and grateful for the support and respect that has already been shown by his loved ones.*

One of those loved ones was Cher, whom Bono called so she could brace for the media firestorm. Much to his relief and joy, she was quite supportive. However, the *National Enquirer* gave quite the opposite slant in an article published on June 19. It read:

> *"When the full weight of [Bono's] transformation to Chaz hit Cher, she*

was reduced to tears and was a wreck *for days,"* disclosed *a friend. "Cher had terrible trouble getting her mind around the physical transformation and addressing [Chaz] as a 'he.' It was one thing for her to have heard about the gender reassignment and quite another for it actually to be* happening. *She is scared for her daughter—worried that the surgery is dangerous."*

Chaz received generally positive responses from most in the media, though he and Elia were forced to put up with photographers staked outside their home. His fear that gay rights organizations would react negatively proved unwarranted. He was praised by nearly everyone for his courage. The attention he received stopped in late June, when the death of pop superstar Michael Jackson refocused media coverage.

Once he had come out as trans, Bono wanted to make friends with other members of the transgender community. He was introduced to Nick Adams, a transgender man who works with GLAAD. Bono's circle of friends with experiences similar to his own grew. They talked

Cher and Chaz Bono appear together at the 23rd Annual GLAAD Media Awards in Los Angeles, California, on April 21, 2012.

about how transitioning had affected their families, how they perceived the media reaction to his change, and how they planned to work politically for the transgender community. They also exchanged stories about the effects of hormone therapy on their bodies. Bono felt that his so-called manly physical traits were developing too slowly and subtly. He was told by others that testosterone injections, rather than the topical dosage of AndroGel, not only provided quicker results but were also cheaper. The switch paid off. Bono grew more hair. Soon his voice lowered as well.

The roller coaster ride that was his relationship with his mother continued, however. In late June 2009, he received a text in which she shared that she was devastated after hearing his new lower voice on a phone message. The reality of his transition had bowled her over. She added that she could not see him for a while. Bono didn't mind. He understood that his mother needed time to come to grips with his new gender expression.

A NEW OUTLOOK ON LIFE

Meanwhile, Bono saved up money for further surgeries. In preparation for surgeries, Bono followed his doctor's suggestion to quit smoking—a bad habit he had had for thirty years. While surgery is a private matter between a patient and doctor, Bono has shared some of his experiences publicly. Bono also took legal steps to change his name and gender on identity documents in May 2010.

However, more important than any change in appearance or legal status was Bono's change in outlook. He had become so happy and confident that he believed himself ready to appear on such noteworthy television shows as *Entertainment Tonight* and *Good Morning America* to speak about his transition and give advice for other members of the transgender community considering transitioning.

The transition opened up a new world for Bono. He met a transgender boy who was just six years old, which led to involvement in a support group for the families of transgender children. The man who once spent his days alone at home and suffered from drug addiction was now a happy social butterfly.

Others were also finally treating him like the man he was, which helped him embrace his true identity. His friends and family could see the change in him. His half-sister Chianna

Maria Bono said that it was much easier to relate to Chaz after his transitioning. His half-brother Elijah Allman told him that he was now living openly as the person he had been all along.

In January 2011, a documentary about Bono's transition titled *Becoming Chaz* premiered at the Sundance Film Festival. The documentary was later nominated for an Emmy Award. A few months after its premiere, Bono published his autobiography *Transition: Becoming Who I Was Always Meant to Be.* Bono and his partner Jennifer Elia appeared on *Piers Morgan Tonigh*t on the CNN news network in May 2011 to promote the book. In the interview, Elia explained that she liked Chaz better after his transition. She shared, "When you have a partner happy in their skin and happy in general...it changes everything."

In the fall of 2011, Bono and Elia became engaged. His proposal was included in a documentary about his life after transitioning titled *Being Chaz* (the follow-up to *Becoming Chaz*). A few months later, in December 2011, the couple broke up after twelve years together.

Bono attends a Q&A following a screening of his Emmy Award-nominated documentary *Becoming Chaz* in Culver City, California, on February 15, 2012.

Bono admits that he feels sadness at times when he thinks about the forty years he spent trying to be somebody who he wasn't. He thinks about his lost youth and how he missed out on many important life experiences. But he also embraces his new world without fear.

In September 2011, Bono accepted an invitation to be a contestant on the reality television show *Dancing with the Stars*. He knew some would criticize him, and he indeed became the target of online jokes and hate messages. But Cher, who had finally accepted and publicly supported her son's transition, had a message for the haters on her Twitter page. "Mothers don't stop getting angry with stupid bigots," she wrote.

Bono's appearance on the show was per-haps most notable because it marked the first time in television history that a transgender man had starred on a show for something unrelated to being transgender. GLAAD's senior director of programs and communica-tions Herndon Graddick released a statement saying that Bono's role on *Dancing with the Stars* is a "tremendous step forward for the public to recognize that transgender people are another wonderful part of the fabric of American culture."

WHEN HE WAS DONE DANCING

Chaz Bono had much to say after his elimination from *Dancing with the Stars* along with professional dance partner Lacey Schwimmer. Some of his remarks were positive, but others were critical. Bono was happy that a transgender man such as himself had been given the fair opportunity.

"I came on this show because I wanted to show America a different kind of man," he said to the cheers of the audience and applause from his fellow contestants. "If there was somebody like me on TV when I was growing up, my whole life would have been different." He then dedicated his appearance on the show to those still struggling with gender dysphoria.

Bono rehearses with his partner Lacey Schwimmer during their time on *Dancing with the Stars* in late 2011.

However, Bono was outspoken that he felt he had been treated unfairly as an overweight person, particularly in regard to comments made by *Dancing with the Stars* judge Bruno Tonioli. "I got a lot of references from [Tonioli] about things that would indicate the fact that I'm overweight...and I just didn't appreciate it," Bono said on *Good Morning America* in October 2011.

Times had changed. Chaz Bono had changed. After forty years, he was happy and comfortable with who he was. In the time since his very public transition, Bono has starred in small theater productions and focused on his physical fitness. Most important, he's focused on his happiness.

TIMELINE

March 4, 1969 Chaz is born to celebrity parents Sonny Bono and Cher. He is assigned female at birth.

1971–1974 *The Sonny & Cher Comedy Hour,* on which a young Chaz makes frequent appearances, is on the air.

1975 Chaz's parents, Sonny and Cher, divorce in June.

1983 Chaz is accepted into the Fiorello H. LaGuardia High School of Music & Art and Performing Arts in New York City.

1987 Chaz comes out to his father as a lesbian, who subsequently tells his mother.

1993 Bono's rock band Ceremony releases its only album, *Hang Out Your Poetry.* Bono begins taking painkiller drugs prescribed for his girlfriend, Joan Stephens, who is fighting non-Hodgkin lymphoma.

February 4, 1994 Joan Stephens dies of pneumonia after a long bout with cancer.

February 1995 In an article in the *Advocate,* Bono comes out of the closet as a lesbian.

1998 Sonny Bono dies in a tragic skiing accident on January 5. Chaz Bono is fired from his job with the Gay and Lesbian Alliance Against Defamation (GLAAD) as his drug addiction worsens. Bono writes *Family Outing,* a guide to help members of the gay and lesbian community come out to family members.

January 20, 2000 Bono checks into a hospital for drug rehab but later falls back into his drug addiction after exiting.

2002 Bono writes a memoir, *The End of Innocence.*

March 7, 2004 Bono checks into a rehab facility in Arizona and finally kicks his prescription drug habit.

July 2008 Bono tells his mother about his plans to transition.

March 2009 Bono begins hormone therapy.

June 11, 2009 Bono releases a statement to the media announcing his transition from female to male.

2011 *Becoming Chaz* premieres at the Sundance Film Festival; it is later nominated for an Emmy Award. In the fall, Bono appears as a contestant on the reality television show *Dancing with the Stars*. Bono and his longtime partner Jennifer Elia break up after twelve years together.

GLOSSARY

ADVERSITY Obstacles or difficulties in life to overcome.

ADVOCATE A person who publicly supports or recommends a particular cause or policy.

AUDITION A tryout in an attempt to be accepted to a school or for a performance.

DISCIPLINARIAN A person who is incredibly strict and uses discipline to punish bad behavior.

DISCRIMINATION Treating someone differently because of a class or group that the person belongs to.

EFFEMINATE Having characteristics or qualities that are societally perceived to be more suited for women than men.

GENDER IDENTITY A person's internal sense of gender often expressed through behavior, clothing, hairstyle, voice, or body characteristics.

HETEROSEXUAL A person physically and sexually attracted to members of the opposite sex.

HOMOPHOBIC Fearful of or discriminatory toward homosexuals.

HORMONES Chemical messengers in the body that trigger certain functions.

IMPERSONATOR An entertainer who pretends to be someone else.

IMPROVISATION An unrehearsed acting performance.

INTERNALIZE To keep one's thoughts or problems to one's self.

LESBIAN A homosexual woman.

LGBTQ An acronym for "Lesbian, Gay, Bisexual,
Transgender, and Queer/Questioning." Also
commonly given as LGBT.

MISCAST To cast an individual in an unsuitable
role.

MONOLOGUE A dramatic or comedic performance given by a single performer.

PROJECT To attribute one's thoughts or feelings to someone else or to an object.

SEXUAL ORIENTATION An individual's sexual
preference or inclination in terms of attraction
toward others or sexual behaviors.

SUBCONSCIOUS Existing in the part of the
mind of which a person is unaware.

TABLOID A gossip magazine or newspaper that
often publishes untruths.

TESTOSTERONE A hormone naturally produced
in the testes or made synthetically that pro-
duces male secondary sex traits.

TRANSGENDER A person whose gender identity is inconsistent with the gender they were
assigned at birth.

TRANSITION The process of changing one's gender expression or presentation that may involve a combination of social, medical, or legal changes, but not necessarily all three.

TRAUMATIZE To cause emotional trauma or upset that has lasting effects.

WORKAHOLIC Someone who works very often, usually beyond reasonable hours.

FOR MORE INFORMATION

Egale: Canada Human Rights Trust
185 Carlton Street
Toronto, ON M5A 2K7
Canada
(888) 204-7777
Website: http://egale.ca
This organization strives to advance human
  rights based on sexual orientation and
  gender identity.

Family Equality Council
1050 17th Street NW, Suite 600
Washington, DC 20036
(617) 502-8700
Website: http://www.familyequality.org
  /get_involved/connect
This organization seeks to change attitudes
  and policies so that families with LGBT
  parents are respected and celebrated.

Gay and Lesbian Alliance against Defamation
(GLAAD)
104 West 29th Street, 4th Floor
New York, NY 10001
(212) 629-3322
Website: http://www.glaad.org
GLAAD promotes positive representations of
  LGBTQ individuals in the media and public

discussion, working to ensure that the rights and dignity of the LGBTQ community are respected.

Gender Spectrum
1271 Washington Avenue, #834
San Leandro, CA, 94577
(510) 788-4412
Website: http://www.genderspectrum.org
Gender Spectrum helps to create gender
    sensitive and inclusive environments for all
    children and teens.

Trans Youth Equality Foundation (TYEF)
P.O. Box 7441
Portland, ME 04112-7441
(207) 478-4087
Website: http://www.transyouthequality.org
This organization provides education, advo-
    cacy, and support for transgender and
    gender non-conforming youth and their
    families.

TransYouth Family Allies (TYFA)
P.O. Box 1471
Holland, MI 49422
(888) 462-8932
Website: http://www.imatyfa.org

This organization empowers young people and their families through support, education, and outreach about gender identity and expression.

Triangle Program
115 Simpson Avenue
Toronto, ON M4K 1A1
Canada
(416) 393-8443
Website: http://triangleprogram.ca
This is Canada's only LGBTQ high school.

WEBSITES

Because of the changing nature of Internet links, Rosen Publishing has developed an online list of websites related to the subject of this book. This site is updated regularly. Please use this link to access the list:

http://www.rosenlinks.com/TGP/bono

FOR FURTHER READING

Anderson, Tim. *Sweet Tooth: A Memoir.* Seattle, WA: Lake Union Publishing, 2014.

Andrews, Arin. *Some Assembly Required: The Not-So-Secret Life of a Transgender Teen.* New York, NY: Simon and Schuster Books for Young Readers, 2014.

Barakiva, Michael. *One Man Guy.* New York, NY: Farrar, Straus and Giroux, 2014.

Belge, Kathy, and Mark Bieschke. *Queer: The Ultimate LGBT Guide for Teens.* San Francisco, CA: Zest Books, 2011.

Craig, Joe. *A Guy's Guide to Sexuality and Sexual Identity in the 21st Century.* New York, NY: Rosen Publishing, 2011.

Farizan, Sara. *Tell Me Again How a Crush Should Feel.* Chapel Hill, NC: Algonquin Young Readers, 2014.

Grinapol, Corinne. *Harvey Milk: Pioneering Gay Politician.* New York, NY: Rosen Publishing, 2015.

Henneberg, Susan. *James Baldwin: Groundbreaking Author and Civil Rights Activist.* New York, NY: Rosen Publishing, 2015.

Hill, Katie Rain. *Rethinking Normal: A Memoir in Transition.* New York, NY: Simon and Schuster Books for Young Readers, 2014.

Hill, Mel Reiff, Joe Mays, and Robin Mack. *The Gender Book.* Savannah, GA: Marshall House Press, 2013.

Hollander, Barbara Gottfried. *Ellen DeGeneres: Television's Funniest Host.* New York, NY: Rosen Publishing, 2015.

Houts, Amy. *Rachel Maddow: Primetime Political Commentator.* New York, NY: Rosen Publishing, 2015.

Huegel, Kelly. *GLBTQ: The Survival Guide for Gay, Lesbian, Bisexual, Transgender and Questioning Teens.* Golden Valley, MN: Free Spirit Publishing, 2011.

Konigsberg, Bill. *Openly Straight.* New York, NY: Arthur A. Levine Books, 2015.

Kuklin, Susan. *Beyond Magenta: Transgender Teens Speak Out.* Somerville, MA: Candlewick, 2015.

Levithan, David. *Boy Meets Boy.* New York, NY: Ember Publishing, 2015.

Nagle, Jeanne. *GLBT Teens and Society.* New York, NY: Rosen Publishing, 2010.

Prince, Liz. *Tomboy: A Graphic Memoir.* San Francisco, CA: Zest Books, 2014.

Scholl, Diana. *We Are the Youth.* New York, NY: Space-Made, 2014.

Watts, Julia. *Secret City.* Tallahassee, FL: Bella Books, 2013.

BIBLIOGRAPHY

BBC News. "Cher Berates 'Bigots' Attack on Son's Role in TV Show." September 2, 2011 (http://www.bbc.com/news/entertainment-arts-14760706).

BBC News. "Cher's Son Now Officially a Man." May 7, 2010 (http://news.bbc.co.uk/2/hi/entertainment/8667595.stm).

Bono, Chastity, with Billie Fitzpatrick. *Family Outing: A Guide to the Coming-Out Process for Gays, Lesbians & Their Families.* New York, NY: Back Bay Books, 1999.

Bono, Chaz, with Billie Fitzpatrick. *Transition: The Story of How I Became a Man.* New York, NY: Dutton, 2011.

CNN. "Bono's Death Caused by Massive Head Injuries." January 6, 1998 (http://www.cnn.com/US/9801/06/bono.accident.pm).

Daily Mail Reporter. "I Prefer Him as a Man: Chaz Bono's Girlfriend Jennifer Elia Speaks Out About His Sex Change as the Pair Discuss Wedding Plans." May 13, 2011 (http://www.dailymail.co.uk/tvshowbiz/article-1386590/I-prefer-man-Chaz-Bonos-girlfriend-Jennifer-Elia-speaks-sex-change-pair-discuss-wedding-plans.html).

Freydkin, Donna. "Chastity Bono Opens Up About Coming Out." CNN Interactive.

October 14, 1998 (http://www.cnn.com
/books/news/9810/14/bono.out.cnn).

Grossberg, Josh. "Cher Sounds Off on Chaz
Bono's DWTS Eliminations, 'Disrespectful'
Judges." Eonline.com. October 27, 2011
(http://www.eonline.com/news/272029
/cher-sounds-off-on-chaz-bono-s-dwts
-elimination-disrespectful-judges).

Hedegaard, Erik: "Chaz Bono: I'm Saving to
Buy a Penis." *Rolling Stone.* January 5, 2012
(http://www.rollingstone.com/movies
/news/chaz-bono-im-saving-to-buy-a-penis
-20120105?page=2).

Krbechek, Randy. "Live Al Stewart." Internet
Archive: Wayback Machine. December 22,
1993 (https://web.archive.org/web
/20090616114924/http://www.psnw.com
:80/~randyk/122293.htm).

Lentati, Sara. "Tennis's Reluctant Transgender
Pioneer." BBC World Service. June 26, 2015
(http://www.bbc.com/news/magazine
-33062241).

Long, Brent. "Ellen DeGeneres Influenced Gay
Rights Views More Than Any Other Celebrity."
Variety. June 30, 2015 (http://variety
.com/2015/tv/news/ellen-degeneres
-gay-rights-gay-marriage-1201531462).

Mitovich, Matt. "Chastity Bono Undergoing

Gender Change." *TV Guide.* June 11, 2009 (http://www.tvguide.com/news/chastity -bono-gender-1006849).

National Enquirer. "Cher Cries for Chaz Bono." June 19, 2009 (http://www .nationalenquirer.com/celebrity/cher -cries-chaz-bono).

Naughty But Nice Rob. "Chaz Bono, Jennifer Elia Split: What Happened?" *Huffington Post.* December 20, 2011 (http://www .huffingtonpost.com/2011/12/20/chaz -bono-jennifer-elia-split-breakup-what -happened_n_1160183.html).

PR Newswire. "OSL Holdings Hires Former GLAAD CEO Herndon Graddick as Chief Marketing and Policy Officer." May 21, 2015 (http://www.prnewswire.com/news -releases/osl-holdings-hires-former-glaad -ceo-herndon-graddick-as-chief-marketing -and-policy-officer-300087105.html).

Sher, Lauren. "Chaz Bono: Dancing with the Stars Judges Treat Overweight Men, Women Differently." ABC News. October 26, 2011 (http://abcnews.go.com/blogs/entertainment /2011/10/chaz-bono-dancing-with-the-stars -judges-treat-overweight-men-women -differently).

Wieder, Judy. "Chastity: Writing From the Heart." *Advocate*. July 9, 2002 (https://books.google.com/books?id=eGQEAAA AMBAJ&pg=PA28&lpg=PA28&dq=Joan+ Stephens+died:+Chaz+Bono&source= bl&ots=1pRlQh4BhE&sig=zDPS9Q6zcw UI18MSAuFvkxByr48&hl=en&sa=X&ved =0CFAQ6AEwCmoVChMIrLno6e75yAIV CPtjCh1muQxk#v=onepage&q=Joan%20Ste-phens%20died%3A%20Chaz%20Bono&f=-false).

Wood, Robin. "Chastity Bono's Memoir." CBS News. June 10, 2002 (http://www.cbsnews.com/news/chastity-bonos-memoir).

YouTube: "Chastity Bono – Could've Been Love – Ceremony." Uploaded November 4, 2008 (https://www.youtube.com/watch?v= Ucugm3L-X-A).

YouTube. "Gender Switch: Chastity Bono to Become Chaz." ABC News. Uploaded June 12, 2009 (https://www.youtube.com/watch?v=w8M_-CJkO2A).

YouTube. "10 Questions for Chaz Bono." *Time*. May 25, 2011 (https://www.youtube.com/watch?v=6CvQ2oKLGE4).

INDEX

ABOUT THE AUTHOR

Martin Gitlin is an educational book writer based in Cleveland, Ohio. His published titles include biographies of Princess Diana, Audrey Hepburn, Chris Rock, Walt Disney, and George S Patton. During his twenty years in the newspaper industry, he won first place for general excellence from the Associated Press in 1996. That organization voted him one of the top four feature writers in the state of Ohio in 2001.

PHOTO CREDITS

Cover, pp. 1, 86 Jason Merritt/Getty Images; pp. 4–5 Gabriel Olsen/Getty Images; pp. 9, 13 CBS Photo Archive/CBS/Getty Images; pp. 18, 41 Ron Galella/Ron Galella Collection/Getty Images; p. 21 © Zuma Press, Inc./Alamy Stock Photo; p. 23 Focus on Sport/Getty Images; pp. 26–27 Barry King/WireImage/Getty Images; pp. 30, 92 © AP Images; p. 37 Allen J. Schaben/Los Angeles Times/Getty Images; p. 39 © Ellen McKnight/Alamy Stock Photo; p. 45 The New York Historical Society/Archive Photos/Getty Images; p. 49 Jim Smeal/Ron Galella Collection/Getty Images; p. 52 Erica Echenberg/Redferns/Getty Images; p. 60 Charley Gallay/Getty Images; p. 62 David Ake/AFP/Getty Images; p. 63 Bob Riha Jr./Archive Photos/Getty Images; p. 72 Scott Gries/Hulton Archive/Getty Images; p. 74 New York Daily News Archive/Getty Images; p. 77 Stephen Shugerman/Getty Images; pp. 81, 83 Bloomberg/Getty Images; p. 90 Beck Starr/FilmMagic/Getty Images; cover and interior pages graphic pattern L. Kramer/Shutterstock.com
Designer: Ellina Litmanovich; Photo Researcher: Carina Finn